Light and Dark

Wendy Madgwick

WAYLAND

Titles in this series:
Up in the Air • Water Play
Magnets and Sparks • Super Sound
Super Materials • Light and Dark
Living Things • On the Move

First published in 1998 by
Wayland (Publishers) Ltd
61 Western Road, Hove,
East Sussex BN3 1JD, England

Series devised by
Tucker Slingsby Ltd,
Berkeley House,
73 Upper Richmond Road,
London SW15 2SZ

Designer: Anita Ruddell
Illustrations: Catherine Ward/
Simon Girling Associates
Photographer: Andrew Sydenham

Picture Acknowledgements: pages 5, 6, and 18 Zefa; page 16 Superstock.

Many thanks to Claire, Kieran, Luke, Poppy and Zachariah.

Words that appear in **bold** in the text are explained in the glossary on page 30.

British Library Cataloguing in Publication Data
Madgwick, Wendy
Light and Dark. - (Science Starters). - Juvenile literature
I. Title

ISBN 0 7502 2163 1

Colour reproduction by Page Turn, Hove
Printed and bound G. Canale & C.S.p.A., Turin

Contents

Looking at light

Light is all around you. This book has lots of fun activities to help you find out about light. Here are some simple rules you should follow before doing an activity.

▶ The Sun is the Earth's main source of light. Night falls when our side of the Earth is in shadow.

• Always tell a grown-up what you are doing. Ask him or her if you can do the activity.
• Always read through the activity before you start. Collect all the materials you will need and put them on a tray. They are listed on page 28.
• Make sure you have enough space to set up your activity.

• Follow the steps carefully.
• Watch what happens carefully.
• Keep a notebook. Draw pictures or write down what you did and what happened.
• Always clear up when you have finished. Wash your hands.
• NEVER stare at the sun. You could hurt your eyes.

Light up

You cannot smell, taste, hear or feel light, but you can see it. We all need light. Without sunlight, the Earth would be dark and green plants could not live. Without green plants, animals could not live.

▲ Sunlight is shining through the clouds. Can you see the light beams? Do they bend or are they straight?

They are straight. Light travels in straight lines.

Making light
All these things make light. How many other things can you think of that make light?

Moving light

In a dark room you can use a torch to find out how light travels.

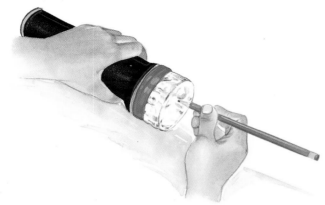

1 Cover the end of a torch with a piece of foil. Tape the foil in place. Make a small hole in the foil with a sharp pencil.

2 Switch on the torch. You should see a thin beam of light. Move the beam around. How far away can you see things? The light travels away from the torch to light up objects far away.

3 See if you can make the light beam hit small objects.

Light travels in straight lines so it is easy to aim the beam. These lines of light are called **rays**.

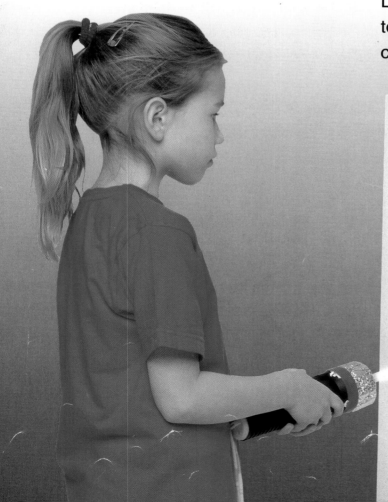

See through

Light can pass through clear materials. We call these materials **transparent**. Some objects do not let any light through. We say they are **opaque**. Cloudy materials that let a little light through are called **translucent**.

Collect lots of objects. Shine the torch through them one by one on to a sheet of paper. Make a chart to show which things let light through, which do not and which let a little light through.

Making shadows

When you shine a light on an opaque object it makes a **shadow**.

1 Draw a bat shape on a piece of card. Cut it out and tape it to a pencil.

2 Shine a torch on to a wall. Ask a friend to hold the bat in front of the light.

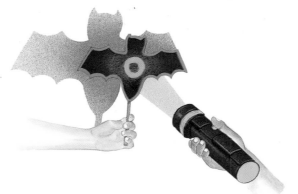

3 Move the bat near the torch. How big is its shadow?

4 Now move the bat further away. Is the shadow bigger or smaller? Shadows are larger the closer an object is to the light source. This is because more light is blocked out.

Shadow play

We can see lots of shadows outside. This is because objects stop sunlight reaching the ground. As the sun moves across the sky, the shadows move too.

Shrinking shadows

early morning

midday

1 Go outside with a friend on a sunny morning. Stand with your back to the sun. Ask your friend to measure your shadow.

2 Do the same at midday and later in the afternoon. Where is your shadow? Is your shadow always the same length? Your shadow always falls on the side away from the sun. It is shorter at midday than in the morning or afternoon.

Shadow clock

Use moving shadows to make a shadow clock.

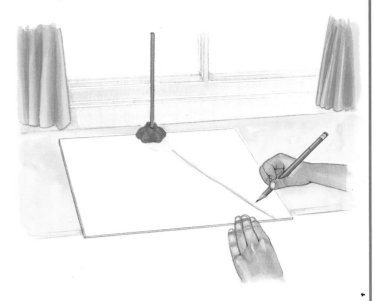

1 Push a stick into some modelling clay. Fix the stick to the edge of a piece of thick white card. This is your shadow clock.

3 Every hour draw a line where the shadow falls. Mark on the time of day.

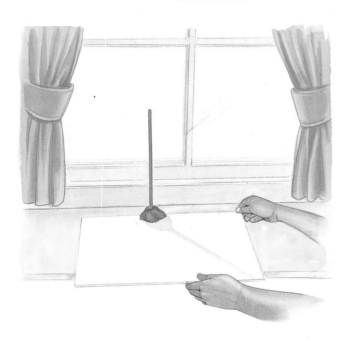

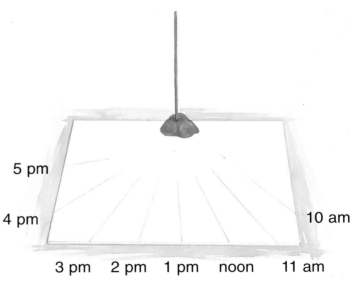

5 pm

4 pm

10 am

3 pm 2 pm 1 pm noon 11 am

2 Put your shadow clock on a sunny windowsill. The stick must be next to the window. A shadow of the stick will fall on to the card.

4 You can now use your shadow clock to tell the time – as long as the sun is shining!

Mirror image

When rays of light hit an object some rays bounce back off. This is called **reflection**. Flat, shiny surfaces make the best reflections.

Look in a mirror. Touch your right ear with your right hand. Which hand and ear are you using in the mirror?

Your reflection is touching the left ear with the left hand.

Light rays bounce off the mirror when they are reflected. The right side appears to be the left side.

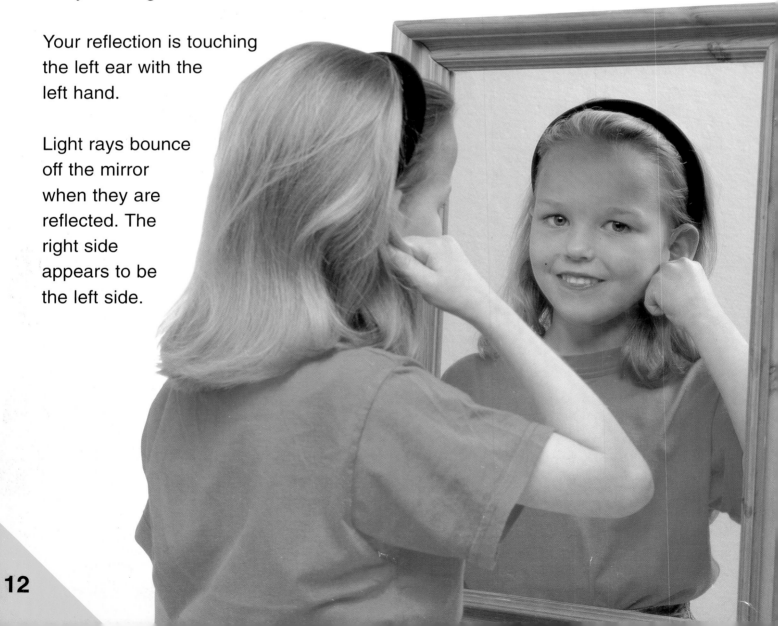

Double up

1 Draw half a butterfly on a piece of paper. Colour and cut it out.

2 Put the straight edge of the butterfly against a mirror. What can you see? The reflection looks like the other half of the butterfly. You can see the whole butterfly.

Time trick

1 Put a sheet of paper on top of the inky side of carbon paper.

2 Draw a clock face on the paper with a cocktail stick.

3 Lift up the paper. The back-to-front clock is on the other side. Now hold the paper up to the mirror to tell the time.

Bending light

Light does not always travel at the same speed. It travels faster in air than in water. As light slows down, it changes direction. The light rays look as if they 'bend'. This is called **refraction**.

Put a straw in a glass of water.
Look down on the straw from above.
Does the straw look straight?
Look through the side of the glass.
Does the straw still look straight?

The straw looks straight from above. It looks broken when you look through the glass and water.

Magic coin

Make a coin 'appear' out of thin air.

1 Tape a coin to the bottom of a plastic bowl.

2 Stand so you can see the coin. Slowly move back until it disappears. Mark the point on the floor.

3 Ask a friend to stand in that spot. Tell him you'll make a coin appear in the bowl. Slowly fill the bowl with water. Your friend will suddenly see the coin.

When the bowl is full of water, the light bends. Your friend can see the coin appear over the edge of the bowl.

Getting bigger

Some transparent materials that refract, or bend, light rays can act as **lenses**. They can make things look bigger or smaller.

▶ Some lenses make things look bigger. The surface of this butterfly's wing looks feathery close up.

A magnifying glass is made from a piece of thick glass. Feel its surface. The glass curves outwards. This lens is called **convex**. Look through the glass at a book. Do the words and pictures look smaller or bigger?

The light bends as it passes through the curved lens. It makes things look bigger. It **magnifies** them.

Jar lens

1 Draw a picture on a piece of paper. Fill a clean glass jar with water.

2 Put the picture behind the jar. Does it look bigger or smaller? The picture looks bigger.

The jar of water makes a curved shape like a convex lens. The jar bends the light rays to make the picture look bigger.

Tiny type!

Some lenses make things look smaller.

Borrow the spectacles of a person who cannot see things well a long way off. Hold the spectacles a little way above a book. Look through the lenses. Do the words look bigger or smaller?

The words should look smaller. These lenses are **concave.**

Rainbow

Sunlight is made up of a mixture of lots of colours. We can see these colours when light splits into a **spectrum**.

▶ A rainbow forms when the sun shines through rain. The same seven colours always appear in the same order.

Make a rainbow

1 Choose a sunny day. Stand a small mirror in a plastic box filled with water. Put the box on a table so that the sun shines on to the mirror.

2 Hold a sheet of white card in front of the mirror. Move the card until the sunlight is reflected on to it. You will see a rainbow. Sunlight bends as it goes through water. Each colour of light bends by a different amount. This means you can see each band of colour.

Spinning colours

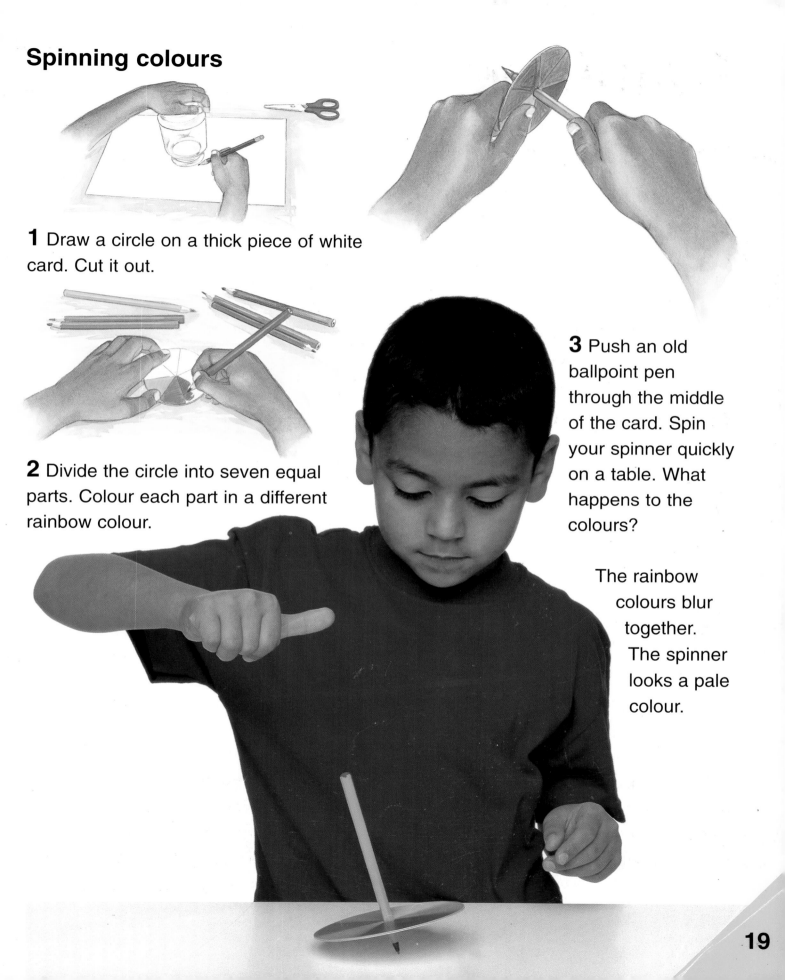

1 Draw a circle on a thick piece of white card. Cut it out.

2 Divide the circle into seven equal parts. Colour each part in a different rainbow colour.

3 Push an old ballpoint pen through the middle of the card. Spin your spinner quickly on a table. What happens to the colours?

The rainbow colours blur together. The spinner looks a pale colour.

Colour code

Most objects do not make light. They reflect the light that falls on them. Coloured objects reflect some colours and soak up the rest. We see the coloured light they reflect.

What colour?

Look at all these things. A white light is shining on them. What colour light does each object reflect?

The red tomato reflects red light so it looks red. The green pepper reflects green light so it looks green. The white plate reflects all the colours so it looks white.
The black paper soaks up the light. It does not reflect a colour so it looks black.

Crazy glasses

Objects look a different colour through a coloured **filter**.

1 Cut a pair of spectacles out of a piece of card.

2 Cut holes for the eyes. Cover them with transparent red sweet wrappers.

3 Make a second pair using green wrappers.

4 Look at some green objects through your green glasses. Now look at them through the red glasses. Does the colour change?

Green things look green with the green glasses. They look dark with the red glasses.

Eyesight

You see with your eyes. A hole in the front of each eye, called the pupil, lets in light. The light carries a picture to the back of your eye. Messages about what you see are carried to your brain.

Hole in the hand!
Can you trick your brain?

1 Hold a cardboard tube to your right eye.

2 Hold the palm of your left hand in front of your left eye. Put it next to the tube about 10 cm away from your eye. What do you see? You should see a hole in your hand!

Bowl eye

Let's find out how the eye works.

1 Cover a glass bowl with a piece of black paper. Tape it in place.

2 Make a hole in the middle of the paper with a pencil. Turn off the lights.

3 Point the covered end of the bowl towards a television. Hold a sheet of white paper behind the bowl.

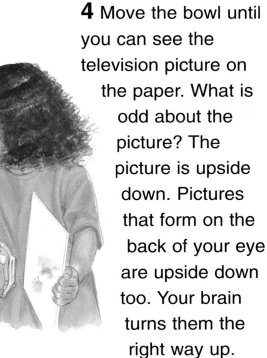

4 Move the bowl until you can see the television picture on the paper. What is odd about the picture? The picture is upside down. Pictures that form on the back of your eye are upside down too. Your brain turns them the right way up.

Moving pictures

Your eyes can only take in 12 pictures every second as single pictures. If there are more than this, your eyes think the pictures are moving. This is how cartoons work.

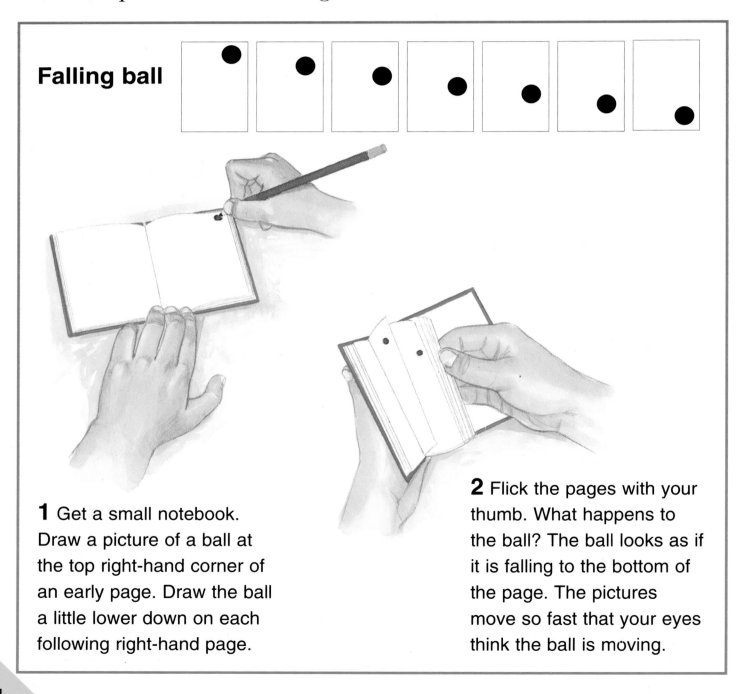

Falling ball

1 Get a small notebook. Draw a picture of a ball at the top right-hand corner of an early page. Draw the ball a little lower down on each following right-hand page.

2 Flick the pages with your thumb. What happens to the ball? The ball looks as if it is falling to the bottom of the page. The pictures move so fast that your eyes think the ball is moving.

24

Swimming octopus

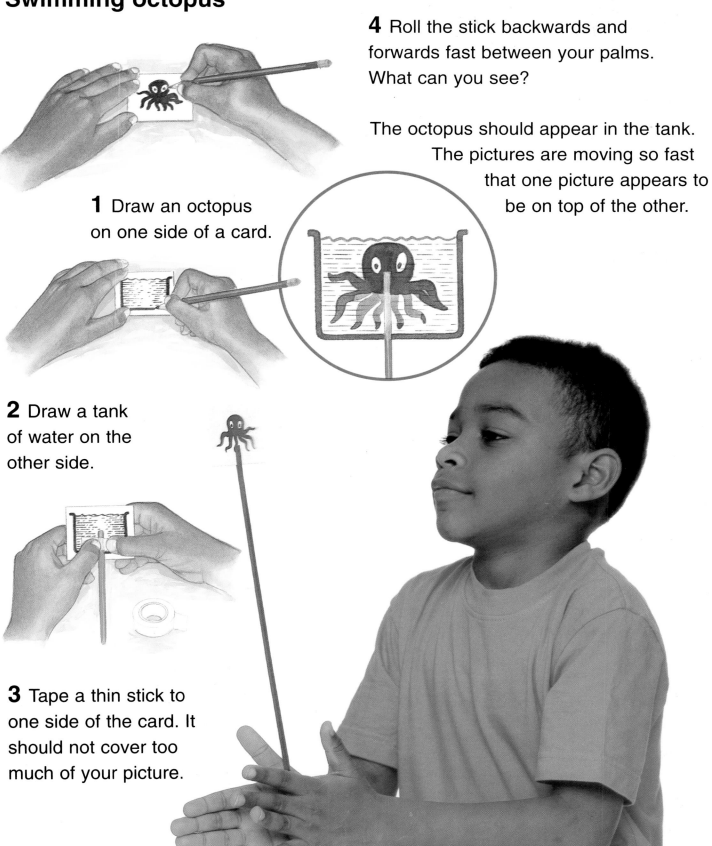

4 Roll the stick backwards and forwards fast between your palms. What can you see?

The octopus should appear in the tank. The pictures are moving so fast that one picture appears to be on top of the other.

1 Draw an octopus on one side of a card.

2 Draw a tank of water on the other side.

3 Tape a thin stick to one side of the card. It should not cover too much of your picture.

Eye openers

Some pictures play tricks on your brain. They are called optical illusions. Have a look at these tricky pictures.

Look at this picture. Do you see two faces or a candlestick? If you look hard you can see them both.

Counting cubes

Can you see two sets of cubes here? Look at the top of the picture and count the cube shapes. Then count from the bottom. One set has six cubes and the other has seven.

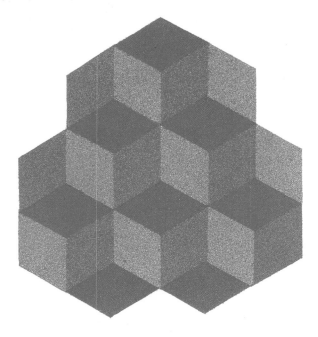

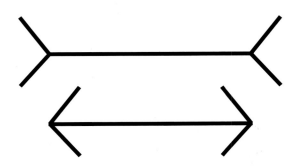

Looking at lines

Is the top black line longer than the lower black line? Measure them!

Blind spot

1 Hold this page about 30 cm in front of your face. Shut your left eye.

2 Stare at the bird with your right eye. You can see the worm too.

3 Slowly move the book towards you. What happens?

The worm will suddenly disappear.

Materials you will need

p. 6 Light up – torch, kitchen foil, sticky tape, sharp pencil.

p. 8 See through – torch, paper, glass, greaseproof paper, coloured plastic, clear plastic, card, pencil, sticky tape, round-ended scissors, a friend to help.

p. 10 Shadow play – metre rule, stick, modelling clay, thick white card, pencil, a friend to help. Choose a sunny day for these activities.

p. 12 Mirror image – mirror, paper, coloured pencils, round-ended scissors, carbon paper, cocktail stick.

p.14 Bending light – straw, glass of water, coin, sticky tape, plastic bowl, jug of water. Ask a friend to help.

p. 16 Getting bigger – magnifying glass, book, clean glass jar filled with water, coloured pencils, paper, spectacles of a short-sighted person, paper, pencil.

p. 18 Rainbow – small mirror, small plastic box, jug of water, white card, seven coloured pencils, ruler, round jar, old ballpoint pen, round-ended scissors. You will need a grown-up to help you make the spinner.

p. 20 Colour code – red tomato, green pepper, white plate, black paper, card, red and green transparent sweet papers, round-ended scissors, sticky tape.

p. 22 Eyesight – cardboard tube from a kitchen roll, glass bowl, black and white paper, sharp pencil, television.

p. 24 Moving pictures – small notebook, pencil, white card, thin stick, round-ended scissors, sticky tape.

Hints to helpers

Pages 6 and 7

Talk about where light comes from. The only natural light source is the Sun. All other light sources use manufactured energy. Discuss how light travels in straight lines and spreads out in all directions. Talk about how fast light travels. Ask the child about thunder and lightning. Discuss which travels faster – light or sound. Light, because you see the flash before you hear the thunder.

Talk about the fact that we need both light and eyes to see. Discuss how the brightness of the light depends on how close we are to the light source.

Pages 8 and 9

Discuss how light can travel through the air and through some materials.

Talk about shadows and explain that they only form if a material does not let all the light through. The more opaque a material is, the darker its shadow. Talk about how shadows change shape and size depending on the position of the light. Discuss the kinds of materials that are not transparent. Some objects stop light getting through by absorbing light and others by reflecting it.

Pages 10 and 11

You must make sure children stand in the same place when measuring the shadows at different times of the day. Talk about the sun moving across the sky during the day. Warn them never to look directly at the sun as it can hurt their eyes. The sun is high in the sky at midday, so the light rays hit the top of your body. This means your body only blocks out a few rays and the shadow is short. The sun is lower in the sky in the morning and afternoon, so the rays of light hit more of your body. This means that you block out more light rays and your shadow is longer.

When making the shadow clock, make sure the stick is upright. Make sure it is kept in the same place. If you can't make the clock outdoors, a south-facing window gives the best results.

Pages 12 and 13

Talk about the kinds of materials in which you can see your reflection. Look at shiny and dull materials. Ask the child how many things they can see in a room that they can use to see themselves. Encourage the child to realise that you can see your reflection in all shiny materials, not just mirrors.

Talk about how light bounces off all objects. Encourage the child to realise that the only reason we can see objects at all is because light travels to an object and bounces off into our eyes.

Pages 14 and 15

Discuss why the straw looks broken. The light is passing through the air then through the water. The light is bent or refracted as it goes into the water because the water slows it down. This makes the straw look broken or bent where it enters the water. Discuss how in a swimming pool things on the bottom look closer than they really are. This is because light is refracted as it leaves the water.

Pages 16 and 17

Discuss how we use lenses in spectacles, cameras, telescopes and microscopes. Glass slows down light rays in the same way as water. This means that the light rays are refracted or bent as they travel into and out of the lens. Talk about the fact that we have lenses in our eyes to help us see things clearly. Discuss why some people need spectacles to improve their sight.

Pages 18 and 19

Link the formation of rainbows with the refraction of light. Discuss how rainbows are formed in raindrops. The sunlight looks white but it slows down as it passes through the water. As it slows down, each colour of light is bent by a different amount. Red light is refracted the most and violet the least. This bending causes the colours to fan out into a rainbow.

The primary colours of light are red, green and blue. Mixing these three colours makes all the other colours in light. Try making spinners with three different colours to see what colours appear to form as the spinner spins round.

Pages 20 and 21

Reinforce the fact that we can only see things because they reflect the light shining on them. An object only has colour because coloured light is reflected from it. The pepper looks green because it reflects mostly green light.

You might need to use two or three sweet wrappers in the glasses to give the 'lenses' the depth of colour required. The green glasses let the green light through, so the pepper still looks green. The red glasses only let red light through. They filter out the green. They stop the green light reaching your eyes. The pepper looks dark.

Pages 22 and 23

Reinforce that you need eyes to see. Encourage children to look at their eyes and see the black pupil in the middle that lets in light. Warn them never to poke things in their eyes as they could damage them. Discuss how we only know what we see because our brain tells us. Use the hole in the hand trick to explain how the brain gets a different picture from each eye. Your right eye sees the inside of the tube. Your left eye sees your hand. The brain cannot decide what is happening, so it puts the two pictures together and you seem to have a hole in your hand.

Page 27

There are no cells that respond to light where the nerve leaves the eye and goes to the brain. So if light hits this part of the eye you cannot see anything. This is called your blind spot. When the worm disappears, the light reflected from it is falling on the blind spot of the right eye.

Glossary

Concave Curves inwards. A concave lens curves inwards. It is thinner in the middle than at the edges. It makes things look smaller.

Convex Curves outwards. A convex lens curves outwards. It is thicker in the middle than at the edges. It makes things look bigger.

Filter A material that stops some things from passing through it, while allowing others through.

Lenses Specially shaped pieces of clear material like glass.

Magnifies Makes things look bigger.

Opaque An object that does not let light pass through it. You cannot see through opaque materials.

Rays Straight lines of light.

Reflection The way light rays bounce off a surface. Most objects reflect some light. Flat, smooth, shiny surfaces reflect light best. They make the best reflections.

Refraction The change of direction of light rays as they pass from one substance to another. For example, light rays bend when they pass from air through water.

Shadow A dark area that forms behind an object when it blocks out light.

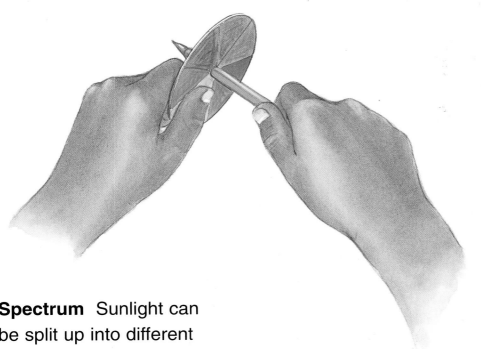

Spectrum Sunlight can be split up into different colours. The colours are always in the same order – red, orange, yellow, green, blue, indigo, and violet. This band of colours is called a spectrum.

Translucent A cloudy material that lets some light through. Things look blurred through a translucent material.

Transparent A clear material that lets light through. You can see objects clearly through transparent materials.

Further reading

Colour by Hilary Devonshire, Science through Art. 1991; Franklin Watts, London.

Colour and Light by Barbara Taylor, Science Starters. 1989; Franklin Watts, London.

Day and Night by Kay Davies and Wendy Oldfield, Starting Science. 1991; Wayland, Hove.

Light by Kay Davies and Wendy Oldfield, Starting Science. 1991; Wayland, Hove.

Take One Day and Night by Daphne Butler. 1994; Wayland, Hove.

Index